AFRICAN AMERICAN EXPLORERS & ADVENTURERS

AFRICAN AMERICAN
EXPLORERS &
ADVENTURERS

EDITED BY JOANNE RANDOLPH

Enslow Publishing
101 W. 23rd Street
Suite 240
New York, NY 10011
USA

enslow.com

PIONEERING
AFRICAN
AMERICANS

Library of Congress Cataloging-in-Publication Data

Names: Randolph, Joanne, editor.
Title: African American Explorers & Adventurers / Edited by Joanne Randolph.
Description: New York, NY : Enslow Publishing, 2018. | Series: Pioneering African Americans | Includes bibliographical references and index. | Audience: Grade 5–8.
Identifiers: LCCN 2017018941 | ISBN 9780766092495 (library bound) | ISBN 9780766093898 (pbk.) | ISBN 9780766093904 (6 pack)
Subjects: LCSH: African American explorers—Biography—Juvenile literature. | Explorers—United States—Biography—Juvenile literature.
Classification: LCC G225.A47 2018 | DDC 910.92/396073—dc23
LC record available at https://lccn.loc.gov/2017018941

Printed in the United States of America

CONTENTS

CHAPTER ONE

CHARTING THE UNKNOWN 6

CHAPTER TWO

FOLLOWING THE HERD 17

CHAPTER THREE

ON THE HIGH SEAS 25

CHAPTER FOUR

IN THE SKIES 35

GLOSSARY 45

FURTHER READING. 46

INDEX 48

CHARTING THE UNKNOWN

From the top of Mount Everest to the deepest recesses of previously unexplored caves, and from the heart of the sea to the sky, African American explorers and adventurers have helped chart the unknown, push the boundaries of the frontier, scale the heights, and shoot for the stars. These courageous adventurers overcame injustice, prejudice, and inequality to triumph in expanding knowledge of the world and notions of what was possible within it.

YORK AND THE AMERICAN WEST

Trekking to the Pacific in the first exploration of the American West was an African American named York (1770–1831). York crossed the continent, from the Mississippi River to the Pacific Ocean and back, as a member of the Corps of Discovery, also known as the Lewis and Clark Expedition (1804–1806). York was a member with a difference, however. Although he was called William Clark's "man servant," he actually was a slave and had been with Clark all his life.

In a time when slaves were not allowed to carry firearms, and when their comfort was not often considered, York carried a gun and rode a horse. And, as a member of the expedition, he was allowed to vote on decisions affecting the group. This would never have happened "back home."

On the expedition, York hunted, fished, cooked, scouted, and cared for those who fell ill. Once, during a flash flood on the Mis-

This hand-colored engraving shows Lewis and Clark meeting with a group of Native Americans during their expedition. York is standing on the right side of the group.

souri River, York's bravery saved Clark's life. York helped in another way, too. The American Indians along the way had never seen anyone of African descent. More than once, the color of York's skin made him fascinating to the Indians. Some historians believe that getting to know York sometimes made the Indians more willing to allow the expedition safe passage through their lands.

Sadly, the freedom and importance given to York on the expedition did not last once the journey ended. York again found himself to be Clark's slave in a world where he was denied the rights he had enjoyed during the trip. He was the only member of the expedition to receive no pay or land.

It took ten years before Clark granted York his wish for freedom. Some say that York died of cholera in Tennessee, and other records suggest that he went back to live with one of the Indian tribes he met on his great journey.

Several geographic sites—including a river canyon—were named in York's honor. On January 17, 2001, President Bill Clinton recognized York for his work on the Lewis and Clark Expedition by naming him an honorary sergeant.

STEPHEN BISHOP AND MAMMOTH CAVE

Twisting and turning in the dark, seventeen-year-old Stephen Bishop (c. 1821–1857), an African American slave, followed the guide through Mammoth Cave in Kentucky in 1838. His owner wanted him to learn to be a guide at the cave. After that first visit, Bishop fell in love with the cave. Spending hours and hours crawling and squirming through narrow tunnels, he discovered more parts of the huge cave system than all the other guides combined.

Wearing a slouch hat, striped pants, and a green jacket, Bishop became a well-known Mammoth Cave guide. He taught himself to read and write. Studying hard, he learned the geology of the cave and loved to tell visitors stories and information. People who traveled hundreds of miles to see the cave waited in line so that Stephen Bishop could be their guide.

Bishop started the naming tradition of caves by using descriptive terms for rooms and structures within the cave. He named one area Chief City after finding things that early American Indians had left behind. But there was one part of Mammoth Cave that especially fascinated Bishop—the Bottomless Pit. He lit scraps of paper and dropped them into the blackness. No one ever saw the bottom. But that didn't stop Stephen Bishop. He and a visitor built a shaky ladder of cedar poles and slowly inched their way across the wide black pit. They had crossed the Bottomless Pit!

The maps that Bishop drew in the 1840s are still used today.

Stephen Bishop's map of Mammoth Cave showed around 10 miles (16 kilometers) of passages in the cave system. He had discovered about half of them himself.

He became internationally known for discovering strange blind fish, snakes, silent crickets, centuries-old Indian sites, and underground rivers. He is considered to be America's first great cave explorer.

AFRICAN AMERICANS IN EARLY CALIFORNIA HISTORY

According to the records, the population of San Francisco in 1848 was only 850. Of the few dozen African Americans who lived in California prior to the Gold Rush (1848–1855), the most famous were "Black" Peter Ranne and Jim Beckwourth (1798–1866). Both were beaver trappers and worked for the Rocky Mountain Fur Company in the 1820s.

Ranne never lived in California as a citizen, but he accompanied Jedediah Smith on his 1827 trapping expedition up the Central Valley of California. The two eventually ended up in Oregon, where Ranne was killed in an ambush by American Indians in 1828.

In the spring of 1850, Beckwourth discovered the lowest mountain pass through the Sierra Nevada range, which made it easier for settlers to migrate west. That pass, a mountain peak, and town are named in his honor.

A third fascinating African American in California history is Allen Light, better known by his nickname, "Black Steward." Sometime in the 1830s, Light arrived in California aboard the Yankee trading vessel *Pilgrim*. In 1835 he jumped ship and became an otter hunter. Four years later, he was commissioned by the Mexican governor of California to police illegal otter hunting in the Santa Barbara area.

The US Postal Service issued a stamp honoring Jim Beckwourth in 1994. Beckwourth was a famous trapper, mountain man, and explorer.

Many other African Americans also distinguished themselves during this period. One was William A. Leidesdorff, a West Indian by birth and of Danish African descent. In 1844 Leidesdorff was granted a thirty-five-thousand-acre parcel of land by Mexican governor Pio Pico. This grant became known as Rancho Rio de Los Americanos and was located in the eastern portion of present-day Sacramento County. Leidesdorff became a successful San Francisco businessman, a town council member, and the town treasurer. He intended to raise cattle on Rancho Rio, but his dreams were never realized. After his death in 1848, portions of the ranch closest to the American River yielded some of the richest gold deposits during the Gold Rush.

MATTHEW HENSON, POLAR EXPLORER

The western frontier wasn't the only one people were exploring. On the morning of April 7, 1909, Robert E. Peary took a flag, fastened it to a staff, and planted it on top of an ice pinnacle. Then he and five men gave three cheers for the Stars and Stripes, flying at last "on top of the world." Chief among Peary's companions was Matthew Alexander Henson, an African American and a key person in one of the most famous expeditions of all time.

Who was Henson, and why did Peary once comment, "I cannot get along without him"? To find out, one must go back to a hat store in Washington, DC, and the spring of 1887. At that time, the US government was trying to build a canal that would link the Atlantic and Pacific oceans. Robert Peary planned to leave for

Matthew Henson sits with other men who went on Peary's polar expedition. He is on the far right.

Nicaragua to see if the canal should be built there. He went into the store of Steinmetz and Sons on G Street to buy a sun helmet. There he mentioned to Mr. Steinmetz that he needed not only a hat but also a personal servant to accompany him to the tropics. The store owner suggested one of his stock boys, Matthew Henson.

Henson was twenty-one years old at the time. His childhood in Charles County, Maryland, had not been easy. Matthew's mother died when he was an infant, and by the time he was eight years old, he was an orphan. Matthew helped support himself by washing dishes in a restaurant. When he turned twelve, he was hired on as a cabin boy on a ship.

The skipper of the ship, Captain Childs, took a special interest in Matthew. He lent him books and helped him learn to read and write. Henson became an able seaman. When Captain Childs died, Henson got a job on another ship, but he left because of poor working conditions and racial prejudice. Henson then tried various jobs that were open to African Americans in those days: stevedore, chauffeur, messenger boy, night watchman, and, finally, stock clerk in Steinmetz's hat store.

Henson joined Peary on the Nicaragua expedition but soon became far more than a servant. He was a jack-of-all-trades, helping to construct Peary's headquarters in the jungle and working on the surveying team. His adaptability, strength, and endurance so impressed Peary that he asked Henson to accompany him to a far different part of the world: the Arctic.

Between 1891 and 1909, Peary led several expeditions to the Arctic. Henson accompanied him on all these trips. Many people of that time were racially prejudiced, and Peary was criticized for taking along a black man, but he found Henson indispensable.

In describing his Arctic expeditions, Peary wrote that the distinctive feature of his plan was "the adoption of Eskimo methods and costume." The native people knew how to survive in the harsh climate of the north, and Peary needed their expertise. Part of his work was to persuade them to help him.

In this task, Henson proved invaluable. He quickly learned the native language and before long spoke it better than anyone else in the expedition. He learned to drive a dog team, hunt and skin a seal, and kill a walrus. Most of all, he won the confidence and friendship

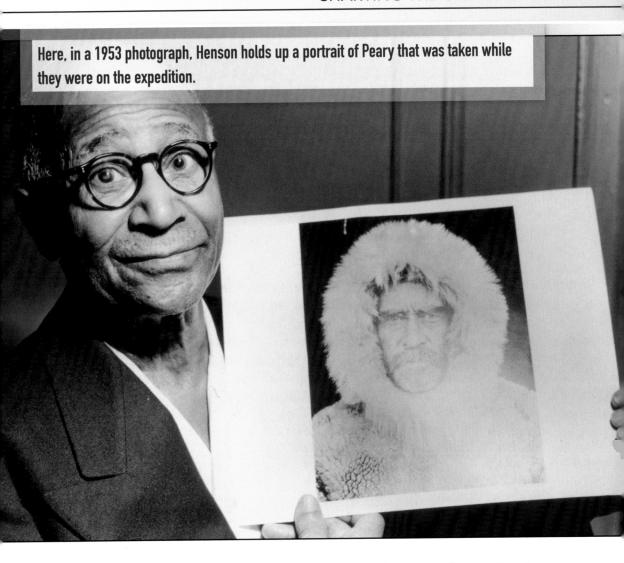

Here, in a 1953 photograph, Henson holds up a portrait of Peary that was taken while they were on the expedition.

of the Inuit. They called him Maripaluk, which means "Dear Little Matthew" or "Matthew the Kind One."

Henson helped in many ways during the expeditions. He once saved Peary's life by shooting an angry musk ox. When Peary's toes were frostbitten in 1901, Henson helped save his feet from gangrene. And frequently he went on ahead to break a trail, risking a fall into one of the treacherous leads that opened in the frozen Arctic Ocean.

After their last polar trip in 1909, Peary and Henson parted ways. Unlike Peary, Henson did not enjoy fame. Although he wrote a book about his adventure—*A Negro Explorer at the North Pole*—he worked as a garage attendant. In 1912 Henson became a messenger boy in the US Customs Department. After forty years of service, he retired with a small pension.

Gradually, Henson began to receive some of the credit due him. In 1945 the US Navy awarded him a medal, and in 1954 President Dwight D. Eisenhower received him and his wife at the White House. A bronze plaque with his picture was installed in the Maryland State House, and a school in Baltimore was named after him.

For some years after his death in 1955, Henson's body lay in a grave in New York City. Then, on April 6, 1988, seventy-nine years after he had stood at the top of the world, Matthew Henson was buried with full military honors next to Robert Peary in Arlington National Cemetery. A group of Inuit were present at the ceremony.

CHAPTER TWO

FOLLOWING THE HERD

For the men who became ranchers and cowboys, the West offered a place for men with a thirst for adventure and independence. Success was measured by talent and skill, not the color of one's skin. For example, Charles Goodnight (1836–1929) was a former Confederate soldier who had returned to cattle ranching in Texas after the Civil War (1861–1865). Initially, Goodnight drove his cattle to places across the South where the beef would be sold as food for American Indians. In 1866 Goodnight and his partner, Oliver Loving (1812–1867), were the first to lead a cattle drive on a route through the Southwest that later became famous as the Goodnight–Loving Trail. Hired to help on that drive was Bose Ikard (c. 1840s–1929).

Ikard had been born into slavery, but after emancipation, he began hiring himself out as a cowboy. In a profession that required loyalty, bravery, honesty, and hard work, Ikard excelled. He quickly became Goodnight's trusted right-hand man on cattle drives, and soon the former slave and the ex-Confederate developed a close personal friendship. Ikard was not the only African American who

A black cowboy sits on his horse in Pocatello, Idaho, in 1903.

chose a life following the herds on the plains of the West. The lifestyle appealed to many men seeking to shrug off the burdens of their race and create a life for themselves.

CALL OF THE OPEN RANGE

Cattle driving was hard work. A drive could take two to three months to complete. Cowhands spent that time alongside the animals, riding twelve hours in the saddle, breathing in the dust the cattle kicked up, and sleeping under the stars at night. They endured all kinds of weather as they guided their herds across raging rivers and through difficult canyons. And they had to be constantly on the alert for stampedes.

Yet, men were drawn to this adventurous life. No one asked questions about a cowboy's past life. Jobs were scarce after the Civil War. Some cowboys were former Civil War soldiers who were looking for an opportunity to put the conflict behind them and start fresh lives. And, with little discrimination in this line of work, approximately eight thousand black men found employment as cowboys. Some, such as Ben Hodges (1856–1929) and Bill Pickett (1870–1932), even became famous for their riding and roping skills.

INVISIBLE HERO: THE BLACK COWBOY

The image of the American cowboy has become synonymous with the West. Yet decades of Hollywood westerns, popular tales, and even operas and classical music have given the world an impression of cowboys that is incorrect in many ways. One major inaccuracy is the absence of black cowboys.

Historian Kenneth Wiggins Porter located lists of trail herd outfits that prove, on the average, cowboys were 63 percent white, 25 percent African American, and about 12 percent Mexican American. A documented 1877 trail outfit listed seven white cowboys, two black cowboys, a black cook, and a Mexican American horse wrangler (a cowboy who herds saddle horses). An 1874 cattle crew was made up entirely of black cowboys with a white trail boss.

Life as a cowboy answered the call for adventure, the need for regular pay, and a chance to live the free life of a "cowpuncher." The nature of the job made it difficult for racism to take hold as it had in many other aspects of American life.

Historical records note that after the Civil War, defeated Texans returned home to find between five and six million cattle roaming the plains of the Lone Star State. Since Texan ex-slaves were already able horsemen, used to working cattle, and looking to earn a living as free men, the newly created job of "cowboy" was attractive to them. Likewise, because they worked cheaply, were already known hands, and had the required skills, they were quickly hired to make the long drives north.

A cowboy's job meant hard and sometimes dangerous hours in the saddle. In addition to possessing a number of special skills, a cowboy had to be courageous and quick thinking. It was often said that a cowboy had to perform while "confronting an enraged bull, swimming a milling herd across a flooded river, or trying to turn a stampede."

The annual cycle of work for the ranch cowboy began with the spring roundup. Cowhands would gather the cattle, brand the calves,

Nat Love is one of the most famous black cowboys in history, probably because of the autobiography he wrote detailing his exploits.

and turn bulls into steers by castrating them. During the summer, the cattle would fatten on the nutritious grasses of the plains. In the fall, another round-up allowed cowpunchers to separate steers from the herd and send them to market. Young female cattle, called heifers, were selected for breeding. Then came the job of trailing the longhorns from Texas to cowtown railroad loading yards, army posts, and Indian reservations. Later trails led directly to stockyards where the cattle would be slaughtered.

Though ranch life was often lonely, it could provide some comforts not often found in a sharecropper's tenant shack. A black cowboy might also enjoy the respect of his fellow cow-hands, occasional equality, membership in an exclusive fraternity, and regular pay.

This 1870 illustration shows cowboys loading cattle onto a train at the Abilene railhead in Kansas.

Because racism generally prevented black cowboys from being trail bosses, becoming a cook was an attractive option. It was the cook who drove the wagon ahead to select the river crossings, pick out the evening camping spot, and prepare the daily meals. Many black cowboys were ex-slaves who had been cooks or kitchen help in the days before emancipation.

Because of their extra responsibilities, cooks made wages that could be as little as five dollars extra per month or as much as twice what a regular cowhand was paid. Although some authors have maintained that cooks were usually not good riders, one black cowboy cook, Jim Perry (1858–1918) of the Texas XIT Ranch, was called by one of his fellow cowpunchers the best cook who ever lived and the best rider in the outfit as well.

A unique task that was assigned to black cowboys quite frequently was guarding the rail boss or rancher and his cash payroll. Charles Goodnight placed the cash proceeds from cattle drives in the care of Bose Ikard. Ikard's large frame and no-nonsense demeanor made him a likely choice. So did the belief that bandits and thieves would least suspect a black cowhand of having this responsibility. Ikard was trusted with as much as twenty thousand dollars at a time and never lost a dime. Goodnight wrote of Ikard, "I have trusted him farther than any other living man. He was my detective, banker, and everything else."

The racism that prevented most black cowboys from gaining promotions to trail boss also prevented many from striking out on their own in the cattle business. There were black cowboys, however, who did buy land and set themselves up as small, independent ranchers. One was Daniel Webster Wallace (1860–1939). After years of working as a cowhand, Wallace bought and operated a ranch that covered a large portion of Mitchel County, Texas.

The level of racism that a black cowboy faced varied from place to place and decade to decade. Occasionally black cowboys were given unpleasant chores no one else wanted. One account even suggested that black cowboys with one outfit had segregated dishes. Yet, according to most accounts, black and white cowhands ate together, slept in the same tents, and were occasionally forced by weather to share the same blankets.

The most pressing type of racism that affected the black cowboy waited for him at the end of the cattle trail. Black cowboys found that their hard-earned money was not always welcome in the saloons, barbershops, and dry goods stores of the cattle towns. In Texas and many other parts of the West, black cowboys could be served only at one end of the bar in saloons. Despite these barriers placed in their way, black cowboys did find opportunities for a dignified life in the West. Dangerous as the black cowboy's job could be, his calling brought challenge, recognition, and an unheard-of degree of closeness with white Americans.

Widespread drought during the summer of 1886, followed by blizzards during the winter of 1887, spelled doom for the careers of many cowboys. As railroad tracks were laid across the West, cattle trains ended the need for long cattle drives.

CHAPTER THREE

ON THE HIGH SEAS

Life as a sailor or a whaler was hard and often dangerous. Yet these same qualities gave opportunities to African American men who were daring enough to take a job that many of their white peers did not want. Indeed, African American men took to the high seas and enjoyed more freedom and success there than many of their shore-bound counterparts.

PAUL CUFFE, MARINER

Paul Cuffe was born in 1759 on Cuttyhunk, a small island off the coast of Massachusetts. His father, Kofi, was an Ashanti (from southern Ghana in West Africa). Kofi had been a slave in West Africa and was sold to owners in America in the early 1720s. He later purchased his freedom. Paul Cuffe's mother was a Wampanoag. Cuffe, along with his nine brothers and sisters, was brought up to follow the religious beliefs of the Society of Friends, or Quakers. Cuffe eventually became a successful whaler, merchant, and ship's captain.

This print shows Paul Cuffe, in silhouette, above a ship docked at a trading port.

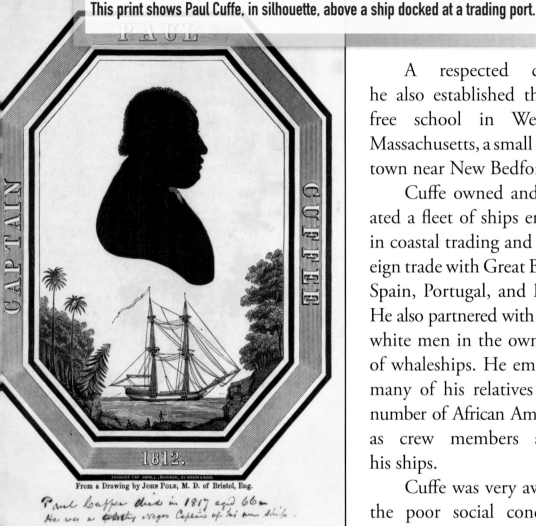

PAUL

CAPTAIN

CUFFE

1812.

ENGRAVED FOR ABRM. L., PENNOCK, BY MASON & MASS.

From a Drawing by JOHN POLE, M. D. of Bristol, Eng.

Paul Caffee died in 1817 aged 66.
He was a ~~worthy~~ negro Captain of his own ship.

A respected citizen, he also established the first free school in Westport, Massachusetts, a small coastal town near New Bedford.

Cuffe owned and operated a fleet of ships engaged in coastal trading and in foreign trade with Great Britain, Spain, Portugal, and Russia. He also partnered with several white men in the ownership of whaleships. He employed many of his relatives and a number of African Americans as crew members aboard his ships.

Cuffe was very aware of the poor social conditions of both the slave and the free African American populations in America. This concern led to a voyage in 1811 to the British colony of Sierra Leone, Africa. His purpose was to evaluate the colony as a resettlement area for freed African American slaves. Cuffe enlisted several prominent Quakers to assist him politically and financially with this resettlement project. During his lifetime, Cuffe managed to transport thirty-eight free African Americans to

Sierra Leone. Before his death in 1817, Cuffe helped to establish several abolitionist and colonization societies in America.

WHALING: A DOUBLE-EDGED SWORD FOR BLACK SOCIETY

Before African Americans were granted citizenship, and before the discovery of petroleum in Pennsylvania brought geysers of crude oil to the surface of the earth, black and white whalers roamed the globe in pursuit of whales. Manning oars and hefting harpoons, they chased the largest living animals and tried to kill them for their oil. "A dead whale or a stove boat!" was the whaler's cry.

Whales, however, did not always die peacefully. Sometimes they fought to the end, smashing whaleboats with their mighty flukes and drowning the whalemen who hunted them. Except for coal mining, whaling was the most dangerous work in America. It was also dirty, smelly, and did not pay well. It took someone with no other options, or with a strong taste for adventure, to take a whaling job.

Whalers thought of themselves as sailors and hunters. They also knew that they were workers aboard floating factory-type ships, separated from shore for months or years at a stretch. The boredom far outweighed the glamour. It was not the sort of work many people wanted, and most of the profit went to skinflint shipowners.

Because whaling was hard and not many people wanted the job, whaleships offered jobs to black men at a time when free blacks faced discrimination in most employment. Black men became vital to the success of American whaling.

Whaling was dangerous work. This engraving shows a whale attacking the harpooning boats and tossing the men into the sea.

For runaway slaves, whaleships also offered a refuge. The crew of the *Abigail,* departing from Sag Harbor, New York, in 1818, included six free black whalers and "Bradford, a runaway negro." In 1842 when a slave named John Thompson fled his master in Maryland, he went straight to New Bedford, Massachusetts, looking for work on a ship. Runaway slaves like Thompson preferred to face the vengeance of angry whales to that of slave masters.

Most black whalers, however, were not runaway slaves. They were young men without wives or children. They made a voyage as a way to earn some cash, test their manhood, or see the world. For a man stuck with odd jobs, a trip aboard a whaling ship held the promise of adventure and distant shores. Black whalers returned with tales from places such as Hawaii, Valparaiso in Chile, and islands off Africa. The work, however, was too oppressive, and most African American whalers never made more than one voyage.

Nevertheless, whaling was the job of choice for a select group of blacks because race seemed to matter less aboard whaleships. "A colored man is only known and looked upon as a man," wrote a veteran black seafarer named William Powell, "and is promoted in rank according to his ability." Thus when the ship *Cavalier* sailed in 1848, at the heyday of whaling, its second mate was a black man. Some seven hundred African Americans then sailed as officers and harpooners on American whaleships, confirming claims that they were the equals of whites.

Even more opportunities for men of color opened up after the Civil War, when the production of petroleum oil forced the decline of whaling. As fewer white men looked to whaling for careers, African Americans and Cape Verdeans received more of the officers' jobs. By the end of the sailing whaleship era—in the early 1900s—those men dominated the industry.

The group of nine islands off the west coast of Africa known as the Cape Verde Islands was an important port of call for vessels crossing the Atlantic Ocean. During the whaling era, the islands were controlled by Portugal. (In 1974 they became independent.) Many Cape Verdeans signed aboard whaleships to fill out the crews. By the 1880s, Cape Verdeans comprised up to 35 percent of the crews in whaleships that sailed from the port of New Bedford. In the years that followed, the percentage continued to increase. A number of Cape Verdeans rose through the ranks to become captains and owners of whaleships.

Whaling is still an unsung chapter in the story of African Americans' creative survival. Seizing opportunities as they could,

This map shows the Cape Verde Islands off the west coast of Africa. Many Cape Verdeans joined whaling crews on ships from the United States.

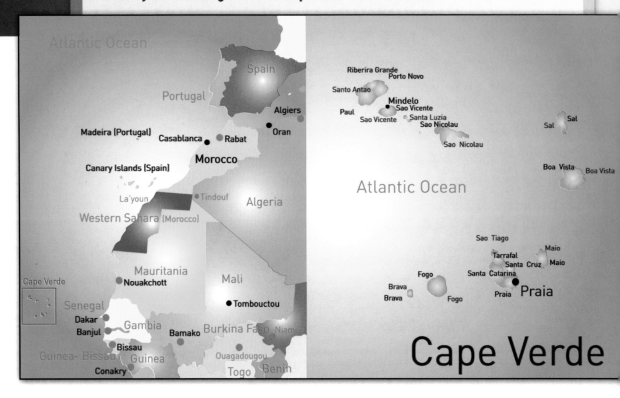

black men contributed significantly to the American whaling industry and—even more importantly—to the development of black society. People regard whales differently today. Whales are no longer seen as prey. However, the indomitable spirit of black whalers still echoes faintly in the sea breeze: "A dead whale or a stove boat!"

CAPTAIN ABSALOM F. BOSTON

Absalom F. Boston was born free on Nantucket, Massachusetts, in 1785. He is the island's only known black whaling captain. He went to sea as early as 1806 and apparently rose through the maritime ranks, acquiring the skills needed to perform in ever more responsible posts. He sailed from Nantucket in May 1822 as captain of his own ship, *Industry*, with an all-black crew. At sea for six months, he returned with seventy barrels of oil and all hands safe. He paid his crew, sold the ship, and remained on land for the rest of his life. He then opened a store and an inn in the area of Nantucket

Brant Point Lighthouse sits at the entrance to Nantucket Harbor. A lighthouse sat on this same spot when Boston went on his whaling trip.

known as New Guinea. A prominent and respected member of the community, Boston was a trustee of the African Baptist Society. The society bought the land on which Nantucket's African School was established in 1824. It is believed that Boston built two houses that still stand near the building and that he lived in one himself. He was also an organizer of the Pleasant Street Baptist Church in 1848.

Boston's daughter, Phebe Ann, graduated from Nantucket High School, which was integrated in response to legal action initiated by Captain Boston. Phebe Ann died a few years later. Boston died in 1855. Public records show that he is buried in the island's black cemetery. His headstone cannot be found, although headstones of other members of the Boston family are there. No descendants of Captain Boston are known to live on the island today.

PARDON COOK, WHALING CAPTAIN

Pardon Cook was one of the few blacks to become a captain before the Civil War. The son of Benjamin Cook of Tiverton, Rhode Island, and Catherine Almy of Dartmouth, Massachusetts, Cook was born in the seacoast village of Westport, Massachusetts, where his parents had established their home.

Cook's father had served as a first mate, the second in command of a ship, on a voyage as early as 1803. In 1812 Cook's sister, Polly, married Paul Cuffe Jr., the son of the noted sea captain, shipbuilder, ship owner, merchant, and navigation instructor. Some eight years later, Pardon Cook married Alice Cuffe, thereby linking himself to the Cuffe family.

On July 12, 1816, at the age of twenty, Cook sailed from Westport as second mate (third in command) on a whaling voyage to the North Atlantic Ocean. Three years later, he sailed on a whaler to the hunting grounds off the Cape Verde Islands, again as second mate. In 1821 he signed on as first mate on a voyage to the grounds off the Western Islands (the Azores).

Once a whaler harpooned a whale, crew members had to bring it on board and process it for storage. These sailors are cutting blubber into pieces.

In 1839 Cook captained his first ship, the brig *Elizabeth*. He had command of the *Elizabeth* on two other voyages, one to the Atlantic Ocean and the other to the "Atlantic Ocean and elsewhere." His last command appears to have been of the *Juno* in 1843 on a voyage to the Indian Ocean.

Cook's crews were all interracial. In 1839 an African American named Asa Wainer was his first mate. On the next two voyages, both his first mate and second mate were African Americans. On the *Juno*, both his first mate and second mate appear to have been nonblack.

It has been said that in addition to possessing nautical skills, a whaling captain had to be a doctor, lawyer, judge, peacemaker, financial agent, taskmaster, and disciplinarian. Cook must also have learned how to handle tragedy and be a morale builder when eleven of his crew were lost overboard after lightning struck a sail on his 1841 voyage.

Within the span of one year, grief overwhelmed the Cook family. In April 1849, Cook's twenty-year-old son, Lysander, a blacksmith by trade, died of typhoid fever. Six months later, he lost a second son, Pardon A. Cook, an eighteen-year-old seaman. Three days later, on October 8, 1849, Cook himself died of typhoid at the age of fifty-three. His seventeen-year-old daughter, Mary Alice, also fell victim to the same fever.

An inventory of his estate showed that he left thirteen acres of land, part ownership of a whaleship, and nautical equipment valued at more than a thousand dollars. Pardon Cook was a career seaman and probably commanded more whaling voyages than any other African American during the heyday of whaling.

CHAPTER FOUR

IN THE SKIES

The world was changing. People were pushing into uncharted territories as far as where they settled, but also in the areas of technology. The country had moved from traveling by horseback or horse-drawn wagons to automobiles, and even to flight in airplanes. There were also changes as African Americans took on more prominent roles in many areas of society. They still faced huge obstacles due to racism and discrimination, which made the pioneering spirits of some amazing African American people all the more impressive as they pursued their dreams to take to the skies.

EUGENE JACQUES BULLARD

Eugene Jacques Bullard was the first known African American male pilot. Bullard was in France in 1914 when Germany invaded that country at the beginning of World War I. He joined the French army and fought in several battles.

Eugene Bullard is shown in his pilot's uniform during World War I.

Bullard then joined the French air force. He flew a biwinged (two-winged) plane made of canvas and wood. He called the plane, whose top speed was only 125 miles (201 kilometers) an hour, a "chicken crate."

On one flight, Bullard had an enemy plane in his gun sight. But before he could shoot down the plane, he was forced to land by fire from German machine guns on the ground. When he checked his plane, he found ninety-six bullet holes. After the United States entered the war, Bullard and some other American pilots tried to transfer to the new US Army Air Corps. Bullard was rejected because he was African American. He eventually returned to the United States where he died in 1961.

BESSIE COLEMAN

Bessie Coleman received her pilot's license in 1921, becoming the first women of African American and Native American heritage to hold this license. She was born into a large family in 1892 in Atlanta, Texas. She attended a segregated, one-room school and later went to college for a short time.

This portrait of Bessie Coleman was taken in 1923, just two years after she got her pilot's license.

In 1918 she moved to Chicago, Illinois. While there, she gained an interest in learning to fly airplanes. However, since blacks and women were not allowed to enroll in flight school, she worked at several jobs to save money. She used her earnings to fly to Paris to attend flight school and got her license there a year later. When she returned to the United States, though, she realized she needed better flying skills to make a living as a pilot. So she returned to Europe to take an advanced course. Once back home, she became an exhibition flyer, performing stunts in airshows. She was called "Queen Bess" and was quite successful.

Coleman hoped to one day open a school for other African Americans who wanted to become pilots, but unfortunately she died in a plane crash in 1926. She had been the passenger in a beat-up plane she had purchased and was having flown home by her mechanic. Despite her untimely death, Coleman inspired African American men and women to follow their dreams.

WILLIAM J. POWELL

In 1927, after Charles Lindbergh made headlines by flying alone across the Atlantic Ocean to Paris, William J. Powell (1897–1942) took his first airplane ride and was hooked. However, even though he had an engineering degree from the University of Illinois, he could not get accepted at any flying school because of his race. He finally found a school in Los Angeles that would accept him. In 1929, with six thousand dollars of his savings, he bought two biplanes and formed the Bessie Coleman Aero Club to teach other African Americans how to fly. He also established the Bessie Coleman

William J. Powell (*right*) formed the Bessie Coleman Aero Club to provide other African Americans with the chance to become pilots.

Flying School and founded Bessie Coleman Aero, the country's first African American–owned airplane building company.

In 1932 a prize of one thousand dollars was offered to the first African American to fly across the United States. Powell decided to try. He was flying "blind" at night, without instruments to tell how high he was, when he crashed into a mountain near El Paso, Texas. He survived the crash and went on to write a book titled *Black Wings* to promote flying among African Americans, as well as to encourage them to become mechanics, engineers, and businessmen in aviation.

39

JAMES HERMAN BANNING

James Herman Banning (1899–1933), a college engineering student who had been rejected by flying schools in Chicago, joined Powell's club. On Labor Day 1931, he flew with the "Seven Blackbirds" in the country's first all–African American air show in Los Angeles. After Powell failed in his transcontinental attempt, Banning and Thomas C. Allen (1907–1989), a young mechanic from Oklahoma who also had joined Powell's club, decided to try for the prize. Unfortunately, they had neither a plane nor the money to buy one. Finally, they found someone to buy them a fourteen-year-old World War I plane with a one-hundred-horsepower engine. Allen said that the plane looked as if "some of the horses were dead."

They decided to sleep at friends' houses at every stop on their trip and planned to "pass the hat" at each stop so that they could buy enough gas to go on to the next one. They called themselves the "Flying Hoboes."

In Pittsburgh, Pennsylvania, supporters of Franklin D. Roosevelt's campaign for president agreed to buy the pilots enough gas to get to New York if they would drop "Vote for Roosevelt" leaflets over the city. In the fall of 1932, Banning and Allen flew over the tall towers of Manhattan, becaming the first African Americans to complete a transcontinental flight. Although the entire trip took three weeks because they had to raise money at each stop to continue, it took forty-one hours and twenty-seven minutes of time in the air to complete the 3,300-mile (5,311-kilometer) flight from Los Angeles, California, to Long Island, New York.

Tragically, on February 5, 1933, Banning died as a passenger in a biplane that crashed during an air show in San Diego.

CORNELIUS COFFEY AND JOHN C. ROBINSON

Two auto mechanics, Cornelius Coffey (1903–1994) and John C. Robinson (1903–1954), entered the Curtiss-Wright Aeronautical School after they threatened to sue the school for discrimination if they were turned away because of their color. When they graduated in 1931, the director declared, "These two young men have proven themselves beyond a doubt. This school will now be open to every Negro student."

Coffey and his wife and fellow pilot, Willa Brown (1906–1992), went on to organize the Coffey School of Aeronautics in suburban Chicago, providing flight instruction to other African American students. When the United States entered World War II in 1941, many of Coffey's graduates became mechanics and fighter pilots in the famous Ninety-Ninth Fighter Squadron and the 332nd "Red Tails" in Italy.

WILLA BROWN

Willa Brown has an impressive number of firsts on her extraordinary list of accomplishments. In 1938 she was the first African American woman to earn a pilot's license in the United States and in 1939 the first to earn a commercial license. In 1941 she was the first African American woman to receive a commission as a lieutenant in the Illinois Civil Air Patrol, which is an auxiliary to the US Air Force and made up of volunteer, civilian pilots. In 1943 she became the

Willa Brown trained pilots for the US Army Air Forces during World War II. This 1941 photo shows her at thirty-one years old.

first woman in the nation to have both a mechanic's license and a commercial pilot's license. And in 1946, she became the first African American woman to run for the US Congress. However, she didn't set out to become a pilot or politician at first.

Willa Beatrice Brown was born in Glasgow, Kentucky, on January 22, 1906. She earned a degree in business from Indiana State Teachers College in 1927 and, ten years later, an MBA from Northwestern University. While working as a high school teacher in Gary, Indiana, Brown felt she had not reached her full potential and sought greater challenges and sources of fulfillment. She decided to take flying lessons with Cornelius Coffey, and later, they married.

Knowing firsthand about the struggles of being African American and a woman and what she was capable of if given the chance, Brown advocated for racial and gender integration of the US Army Air Corps, among other causes, throughout her career.

JAMES PECK

In 1937 James Peck (1912–1996), a young African American from Pittsburgh, slipped secretly into Spain to fight in the Spanish Civil War. In a book titled *Armies with Wings,* he described his first experience in aerial combat where he had earned a victory. He would be credited with four more, becoming the world's first African American ace (a military pilot who has destroyed five or more enemy aircraft).

All these pioneers helped pave the way for the Tuskegee Airmen and the others who followed. The Tuskagee Airmen, one of the most respected squadrons of World World II, proved that African Americans could operate and maintain complex military aircraft.

This photograph of one of the classes of Tuskegee Airmen was taken in 1942.

The Army Air Corps (AAC) was first established in 1926 as an extension of the army. In 1941 it became the Army Air Forces. It was not until 1947 that the United States Air Force became an independent arm of the military. And on July 26, 1948, President Harry S. Truman issued an executive order to end racial discrimination in the US Armed Forces.

brig A two-masted ship that has square sails, or rigging, on both masts.

corps A group of people working for the same organization and toward the same goal.

cowpuncher A cowboy.

demeanor Outward appearance or way of holding oneself.

discrimination Unjust or unfair treatment of people, especially in relation to race, gender, or religion.

first mate The person who is second in command to the master of a ship.

frontier Unexplored land or wilderness.

oppressive Causing depression, low spirits, or physical and mental discomfort.

pension A regular payment made to someone in retirement by the person's onetime employer.

refuge A place that provides safety and shelter.

second mate The person who is third in command to the master of a ship.

segregated Separated from others, often due to racial or religious differences.

stevedore A person hired to load and unload cargo from ships.

stove Damaged.

typhoid fever An infectious fever that is characterized by red spots that form on a person's chest, and stomach and intestinal upset and pain.

FURTHER READING

BOOKS

Gabridge, Patrick. *Steering to Freedom.* Tucson, AZ: Penmore Press, 2015.

Greenly, Larry. *Eugene Bullard: World's First Black Fighter Pilot.* Montgomery, AL: NewSouth Books, 2013.

Henson, Matthew A. *A Journey for the Ages: Matthew Henson and Robert Peary's Historic North Pole Expedition.* New York, NY: Skyhorse Publishing, 2016.

Sanford, William R., and Carl R. Green. *Bill Pickett: Courageous African-American Cowboy.* Berkeley Heights, NJ: Enslow Publishers, 2012.

Small, Cathleen. *Bessie Coleman: First Female African American and Native American Pilot.* New York, NY: Cavendish Square Publishing, 2017.

Tucker, Philip Thomas. *Father of the Tuskegee Airmen, John C. Robinson.* Washington, DC: Potomac Books, 2012.

WEBSITES

BlackPast.org

www.blackpast.org/

An online guide to African American history, including "101 African American Firsts," primary documents, major speeches, and historical timelines.

PBS.org

www.pbs.org/lewisandclark/inside/york.html

Lewis and Clark: The Journey of the Corpse of Discovery provides an article on York as well as a timeline, maps, journal entries, and interactive activities related to the expedition.

Smithsonian.com

www.smithsonianmag.com/history/lesser-known-history-african-american-cowboys-180962144/

Dive deeper into the history of the black cowboys.

INDEX

A
Allen, Thomas C., 40
Arctic exploration, 12, 14

B
Banning, James Herman, 40
Beckwourth, Jim, 10
Bishop, Stephen, 8–9, 10
Boston, Absalom F., 30–32
Brown, Willa, 41, 43
Bullard, Eugene Jacques, 35, 36

C
California history, 10, 12
Cape Verdeans, 29
cattle driving, 17, 19, 20, 24
cave exploration, 8, 9, 10
Civil War, 17, 19, 20, 29, 32
Coffey, Cornelius, 41, 43
Coleman, Bessie, 37, 38

Cook, Pardon, 32, 33, 34
cooks, 20, 23
cowboys, 19, 20, 22, 23, 24
Cuffe, Paul, 25, 26–27, 32

D
discrimination, 19, 27, 35, 38, 41, 44

G
Goodnight, Charles, 17, 23

H
Henson, Matthew Alexander, 12, 13–14, 15, 16
Hodges, Ben, 19

I
Ikard, Bose, 17, 23

L
Leidesdorff, William A., 12
Lewis and Clark Expedition, 6, 7, 8

Light, Allen "Black Steward," 10

P
Peary, Robert, 12–13, 14, 15, 16
Peck, James, 43
Perry, Jim, 23
Pickett, Bill, 19
pilots, 35, 36, 37, 38, 39, 40, 41, 43
Powell, William J., 38–39

R
racism, 22–23, 24, 35
Ranne, Peter, 10
Robinson, John C., 41

T
Thompson, John, 28

W
Wallace, Daniel Webster, 23
whaling, 27, 28, 29, 30, 31, 33, 34

Y
York, 6–7, 8